Ayr Ontario in Colour Photos, Saving Our History One Photo at a Time

Photography
by Barbara Raué
2015

Series Name:
Cruising Ontario

Book 98: Ayr

Cover photo: 99 Stanley Street,
Queen's Restaurant and Tavern

Series Name: Cruising Ontario
Saving Our History One Photo at a Time
in colour photos

Other Books by Barbara Raue

Coins of Gold

Arrows, Indians and Love

The Life and Times of Barbara
Volume 1: Inventions That Have Enhanced My Life
Volume 2: Entertainment That I Have Enjoyed
Volume 3: East Coast Trips
Volume 4: Olympics Have Always Intrigued Me
Volume 5: Wonders of the World
Volume 6: Caribbean Cruises We Have Enjoyed
Volume 7: Animals
Volume 8: Storms and Other Major Disasters in My Lifetime
Volume 9: Wars, Terrorist Attacks and Major Disasters

The Cromwell Family Book

Laura Secord Discovered

Visit Barbara's website to view all of her books
http://barbararaue.ca

Ayr

Ayr is located south of Kitchener and west of Cambridge, and south of Highway 401.

In 1824, Abel Mudge built a saw mill and flour mill at the junction of Cedar Creek and the Nith River. This was the first of three settlements, Jedburgh in the east (Main Street), Nithvale in the west (Piper Street) and Mudge's Mill in the centre (Stanley/Northumberland Streets) in what is today the Village of Ayr.

Jedburgh began in 1832 when John Hall, a young immigrant from Jedburgh, Scotland, purchased a 75-acre parcel of land that included the area now flooded by Jedburgh Dam. By 1850 Hall had developed several industries, including a flour mill, sawmill and distillery with water power provided by the damming of Cedar Creek. At the same time a smaller settlement, Nithvale, was founded to the west of Mudge's Mill where a small sawmill opened along the Nith River.

In 1840 when Robert Wyllie established a post office it was given the name "Ayr", a name influenced by the large number of former Ayrshire, Scotland immigrants who were drawn to Canada by promises of inexpensive, fertile land.

In 1846–47 Daniel Manley's mill was built, William Baker's store was established and John Watson's foundry constructed with Watson's Dam its power reservoir. These three key businesses played large roles in Ayr's early success as did the coming of the Credit Valley Railway in 1879. James Somerville began the first Ayr newspaper in 1854.

Table of Contents

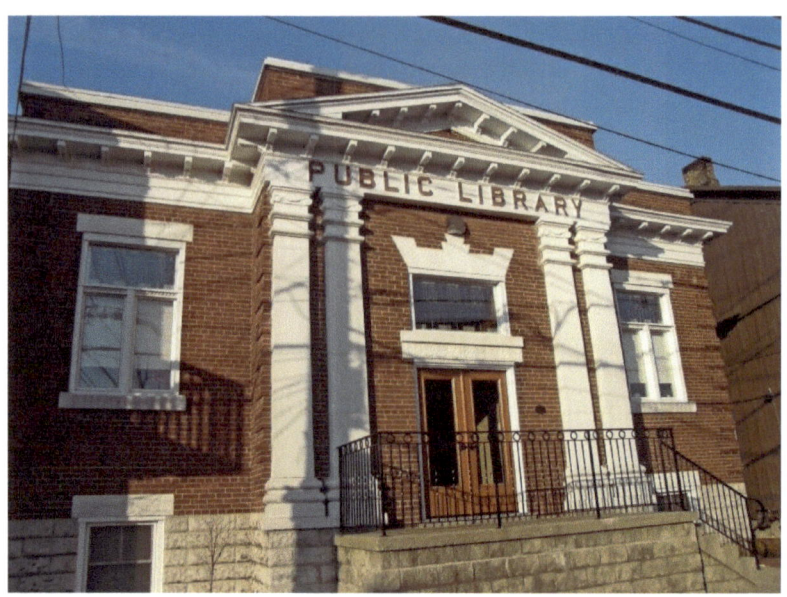

A subscription library was started in Ayr in the 1840s. Andrew Carnegie was asked for a grant to build a library and in 1909 Ayr became the smallest community in Ontario to receive a Carnegie grant. In 1911, the library moved into the building at 92 Stanley Street where it remained for 94 years. In 2004, the library moved into a newer 7,000-square-foot building at 137 Stanley Street, leaving this neoclassical building vacant.

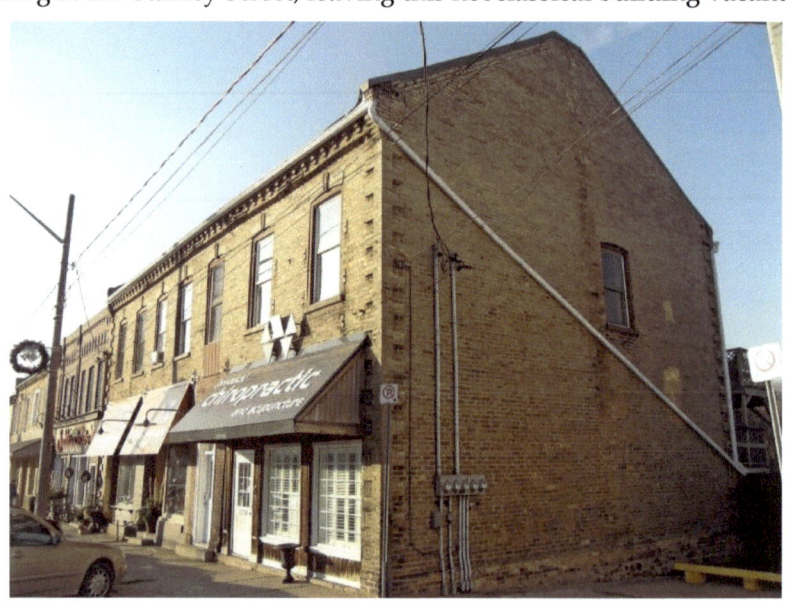

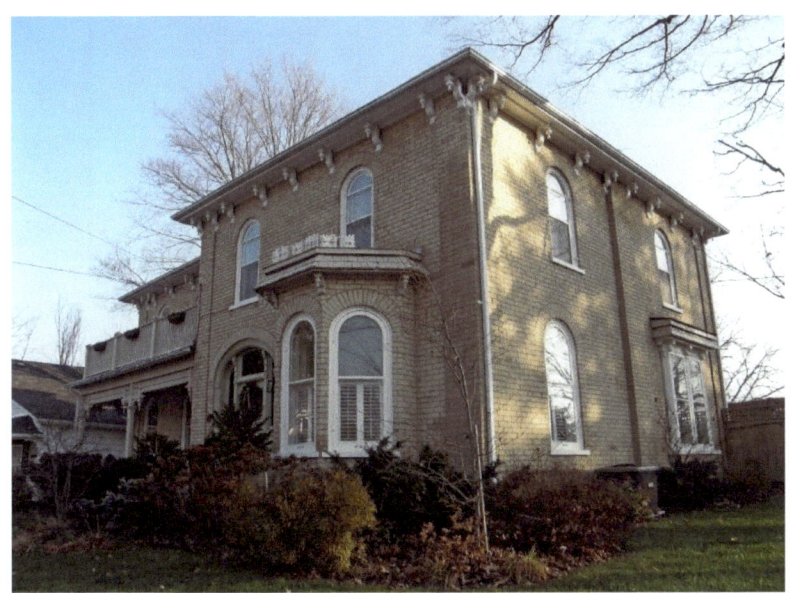

Italianate - single cornice brackets,
iron cresting above bay window

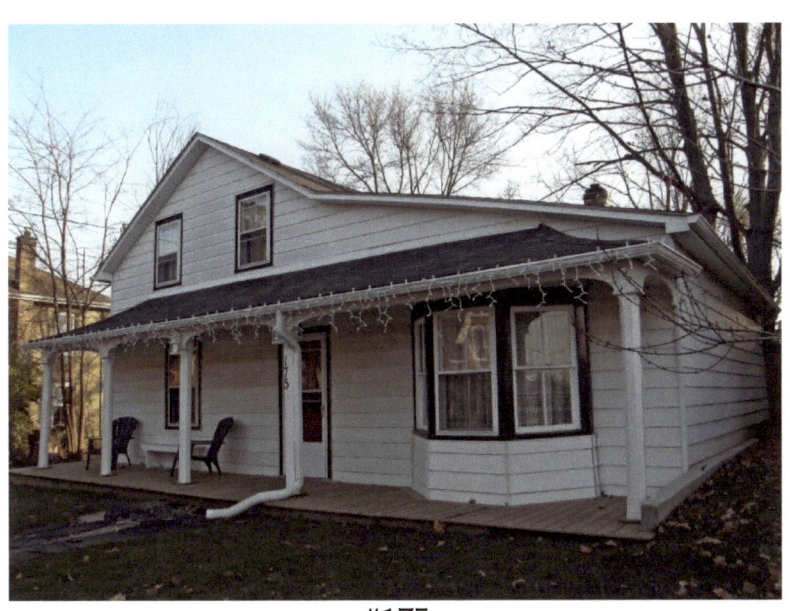

#175

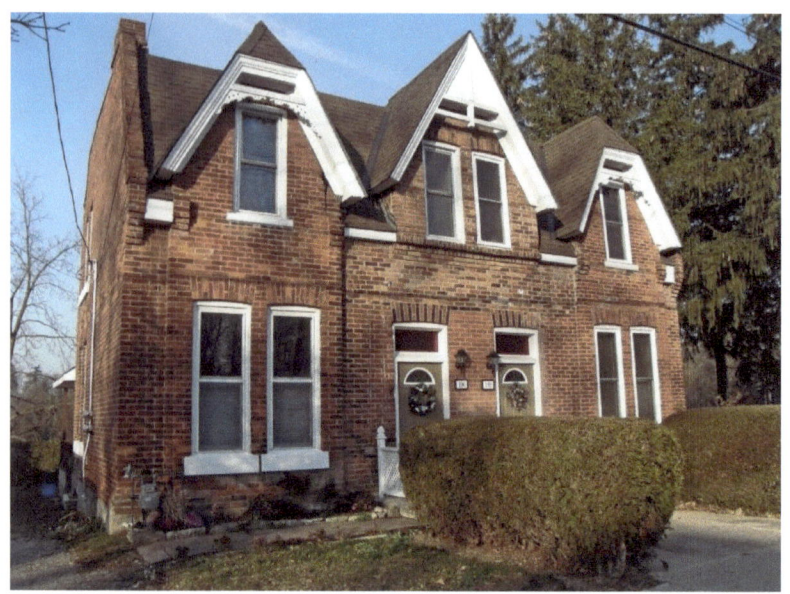

Triple-gable Gothic Revival style - #190 and #192

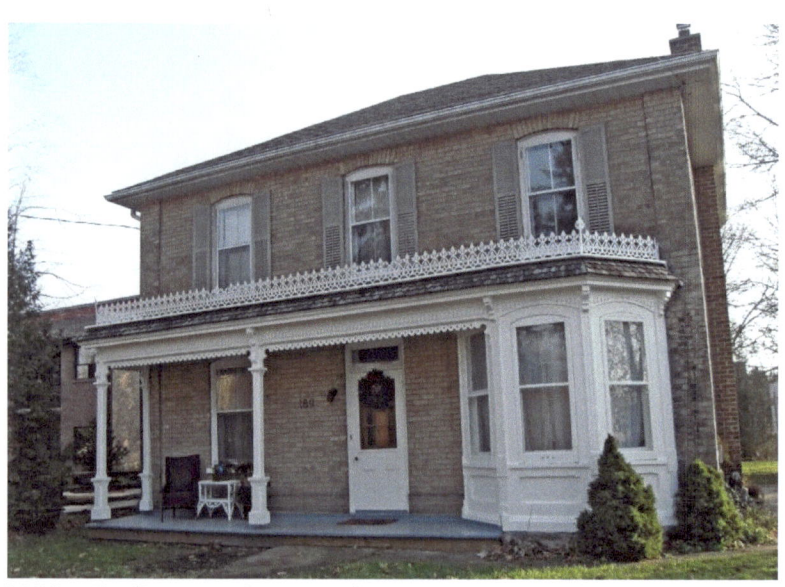

#189 – Italianate, hip roof, iron cresting above verandah

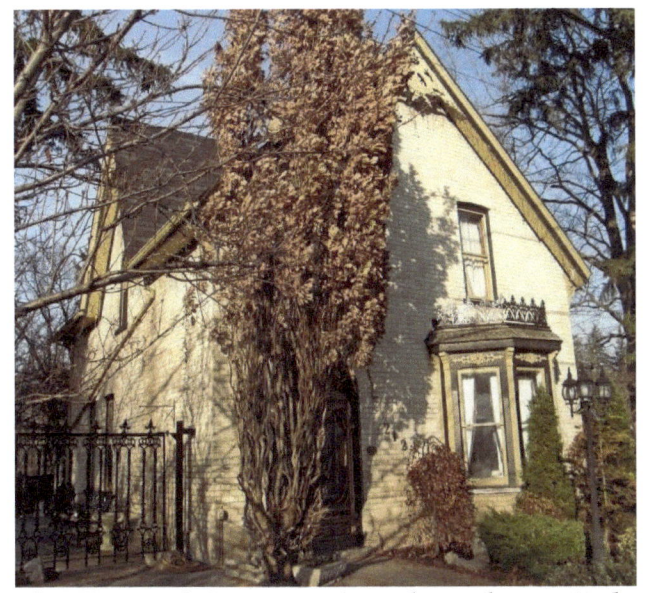

Gothic Revival, iron cresting above bay window,
Verge board on gable

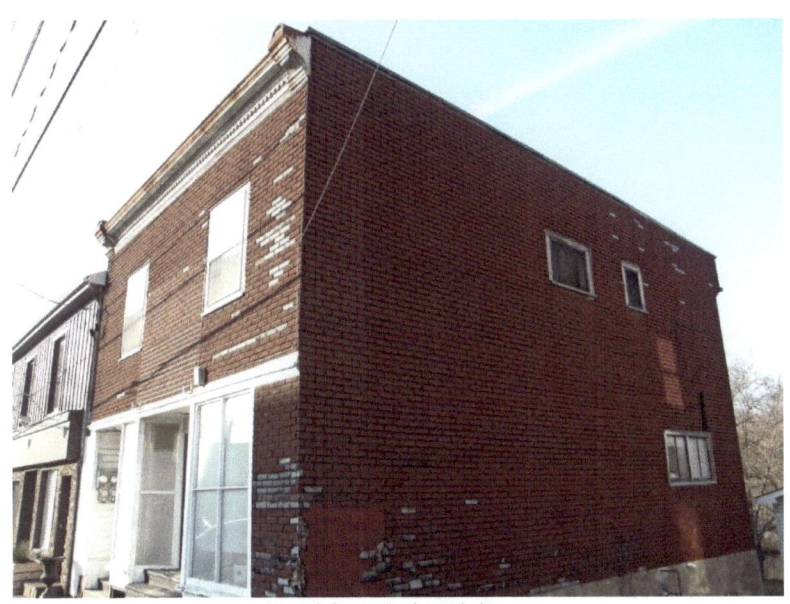

Red brick building

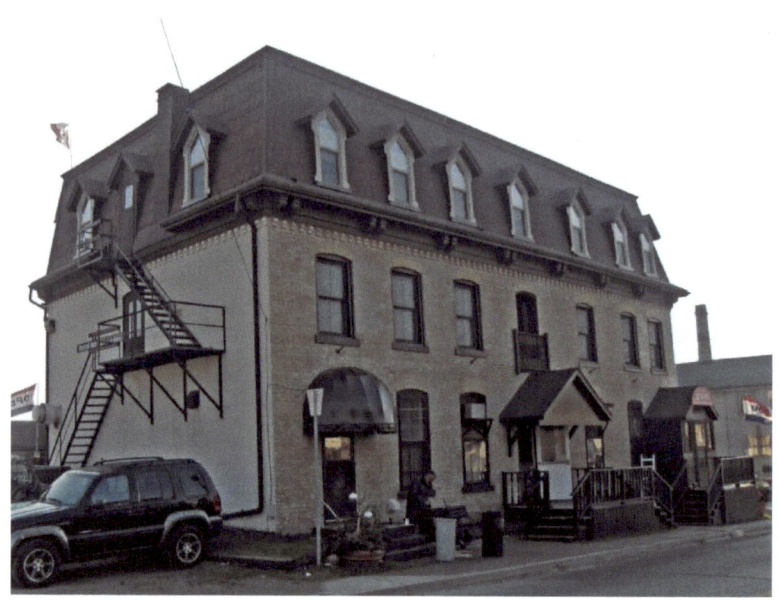

99 Stanley Street - Queen's Restaurant and Tavern since 1856,
Second Empire style, mansard roof, dormers,
paired cornice brackets, dentil moulding

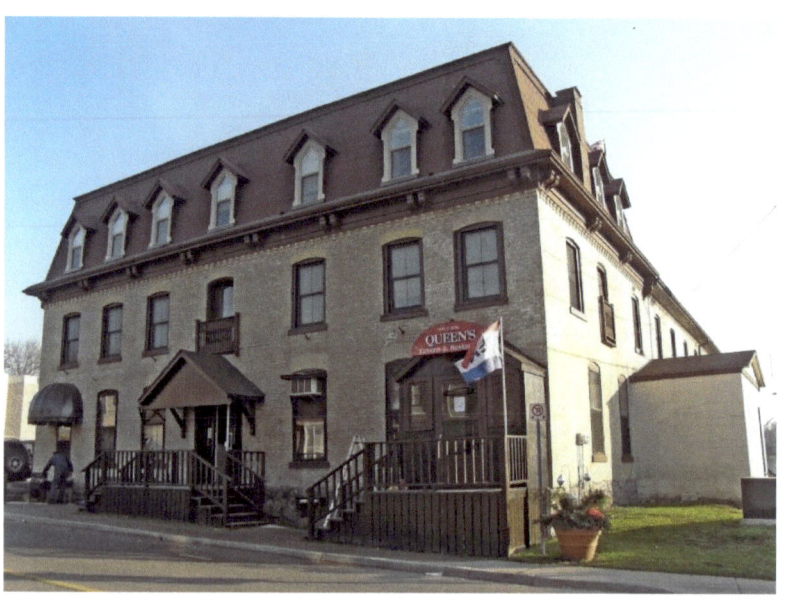

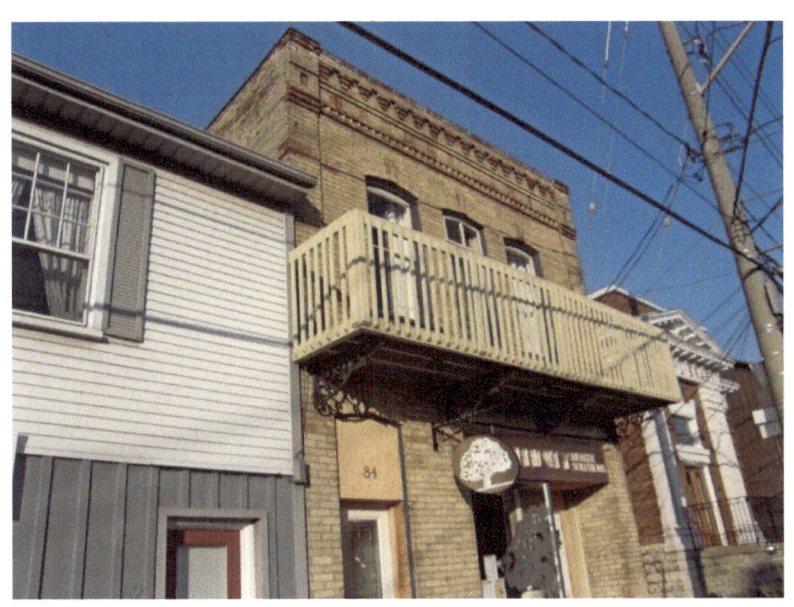

Dichromatic brickwork, bevelled dentil moulding

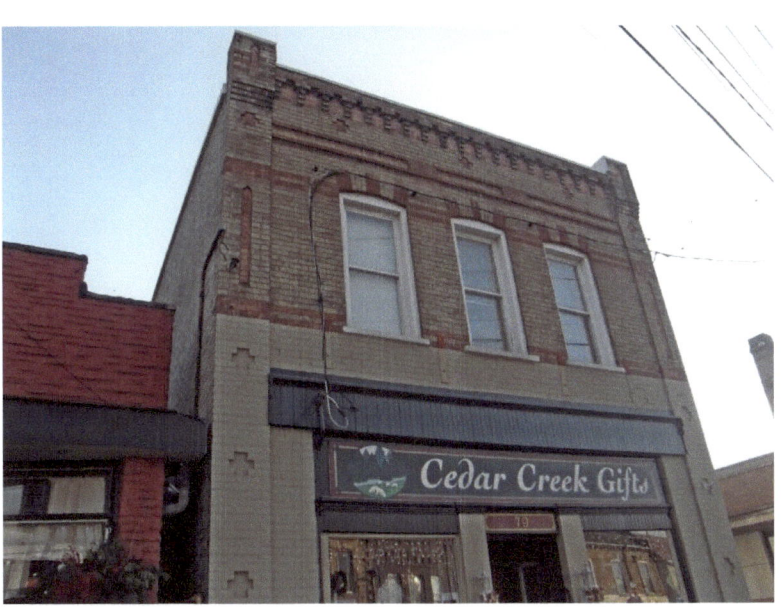

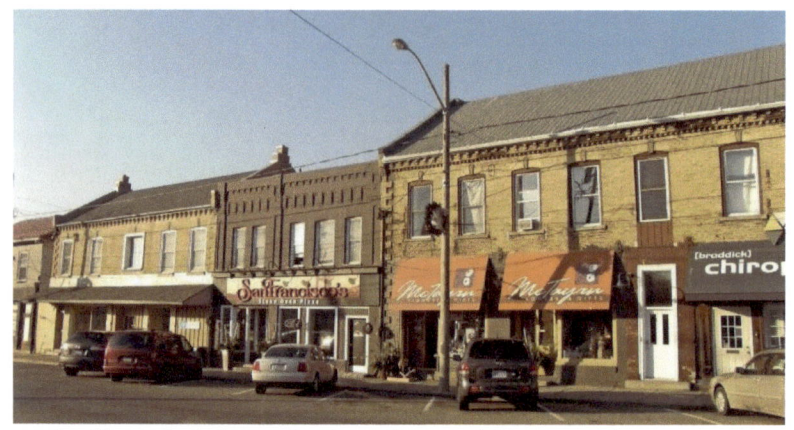

Yellow brick with dentil moulding under eaves,
keystones above windows

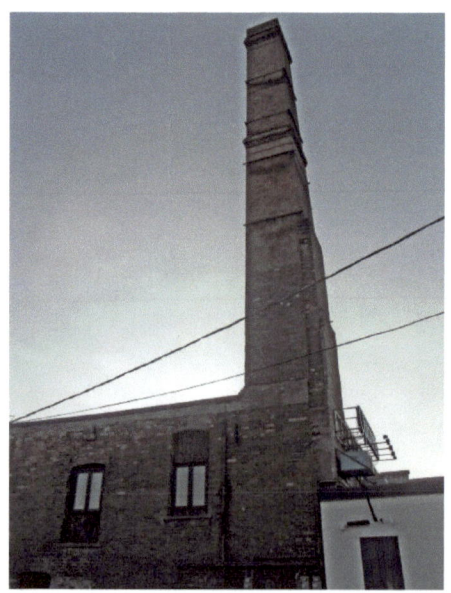

The John Watson Manufacturing Company

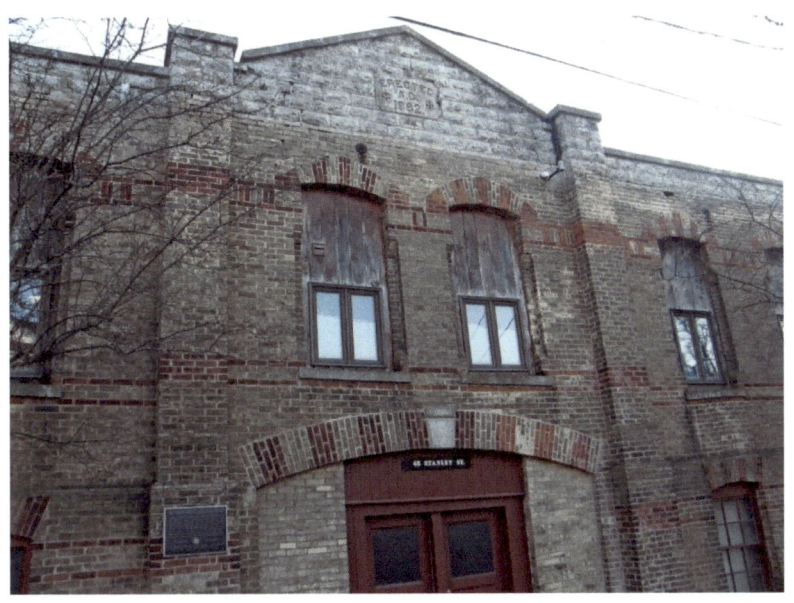

The John Watson Manufacturing Company was founded in 1847 by John Watson, a Scottish moulder and first reeve of Ayr. This building was built in 1882. In continuous family operation for over 127 years, the foundry originally made cast iron pots but expanded into agricultural machinery in the 1880s. It became the largest and best equipped agricultural works in Canada. Over 40 different implements were manufactured with many winning prizes at international exhibitions. Water power was used from 1884 to 1970. In 1920, a fire destroyed the factory and the present two-storey factory was rebuilt from the remains of the original facility.

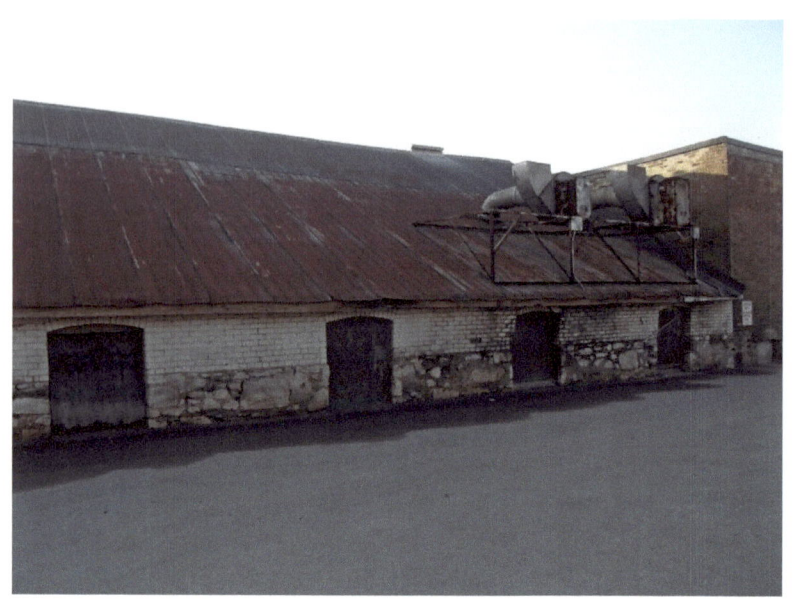

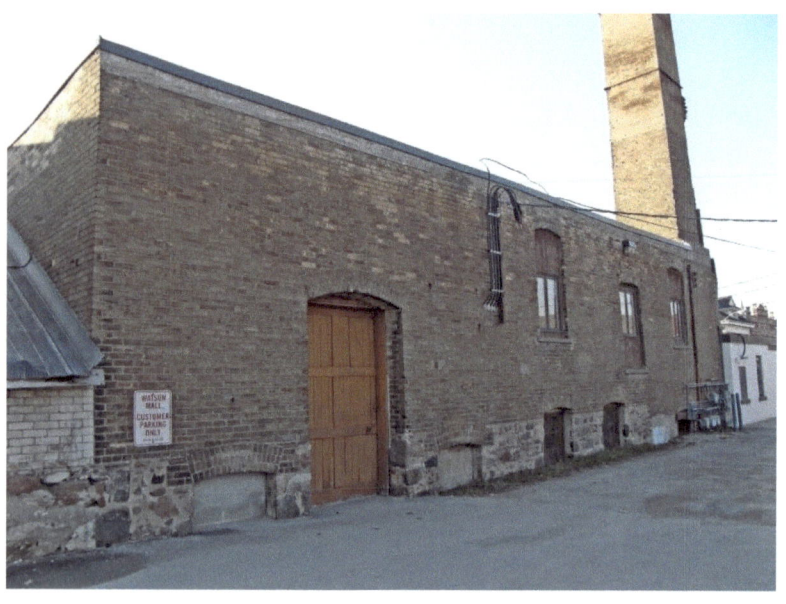

14

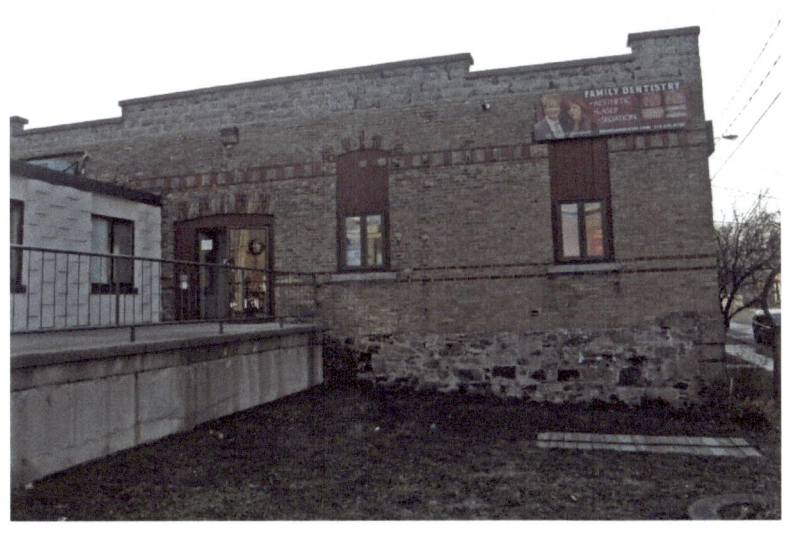

Dichromatic brickwork, cobblestone basement wall

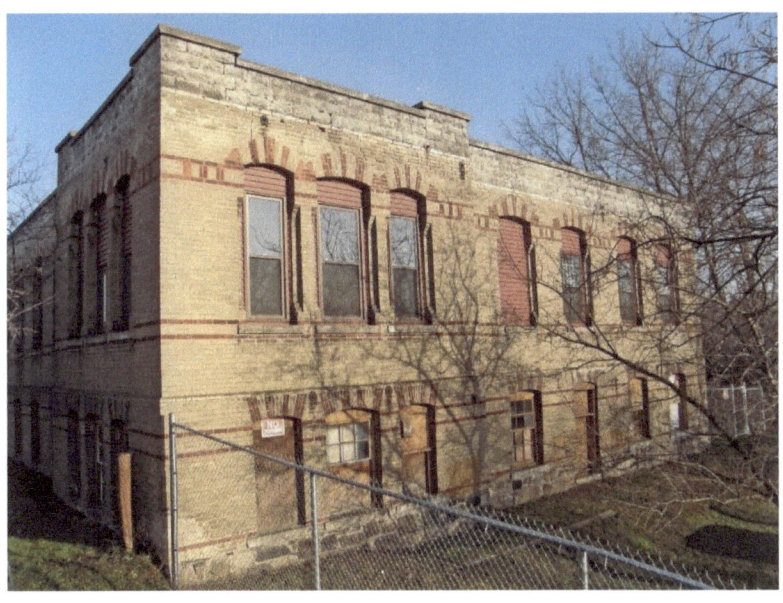

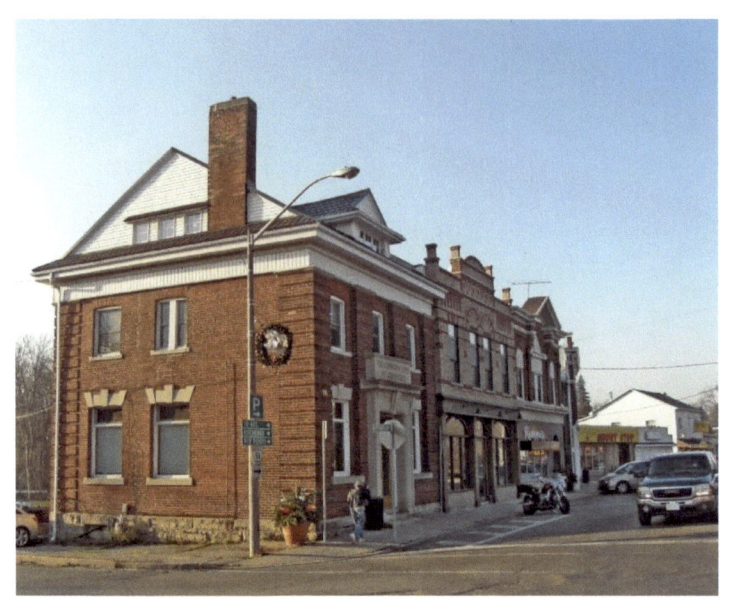

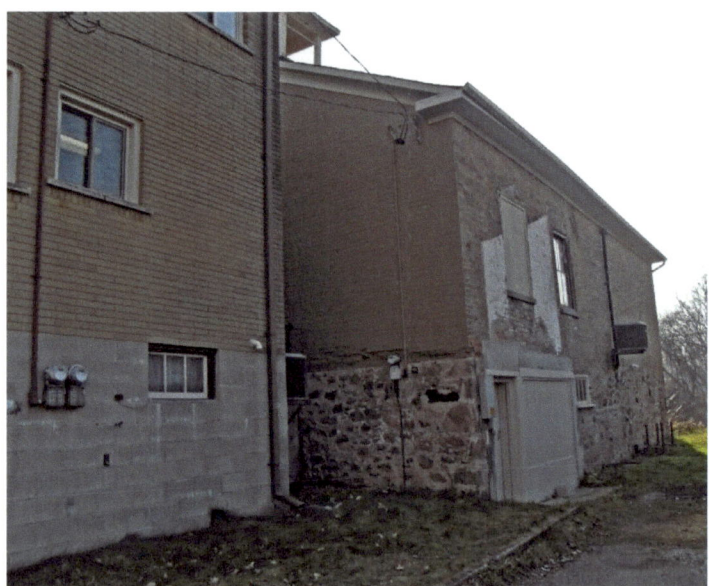

Cobblestone basement wall

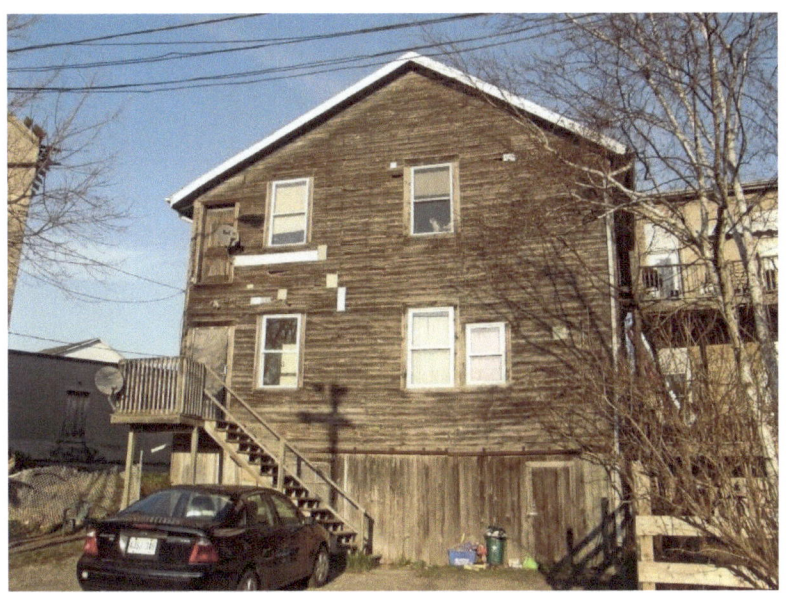

Cedar planking

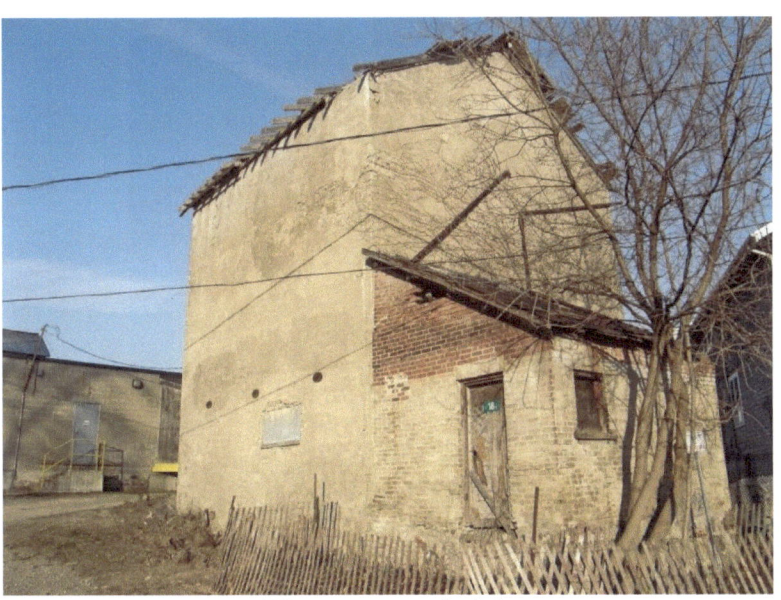

Plaster over brick

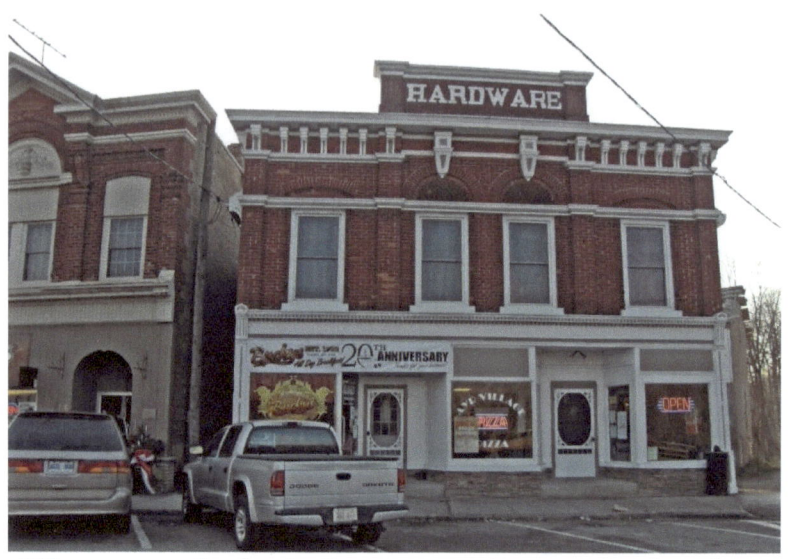

Pilasters, arched window voussoirs, cornice brackets

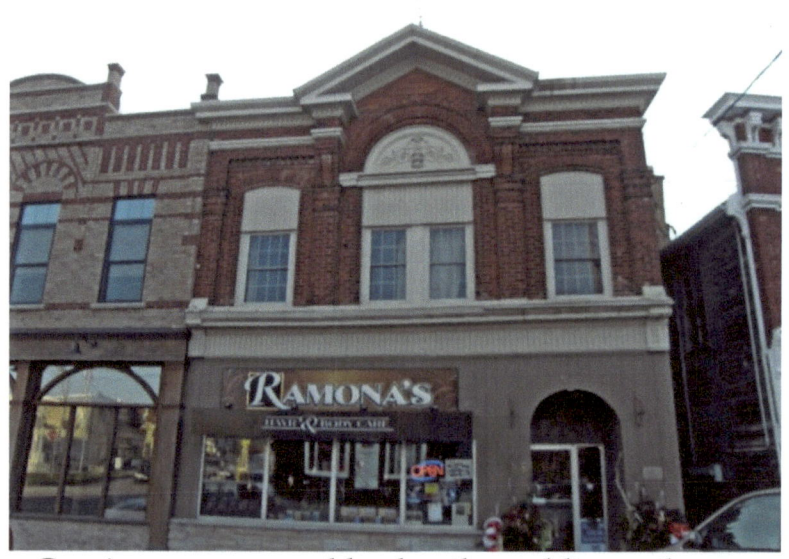

Cornice return on gable, dentil moulding, pilasters

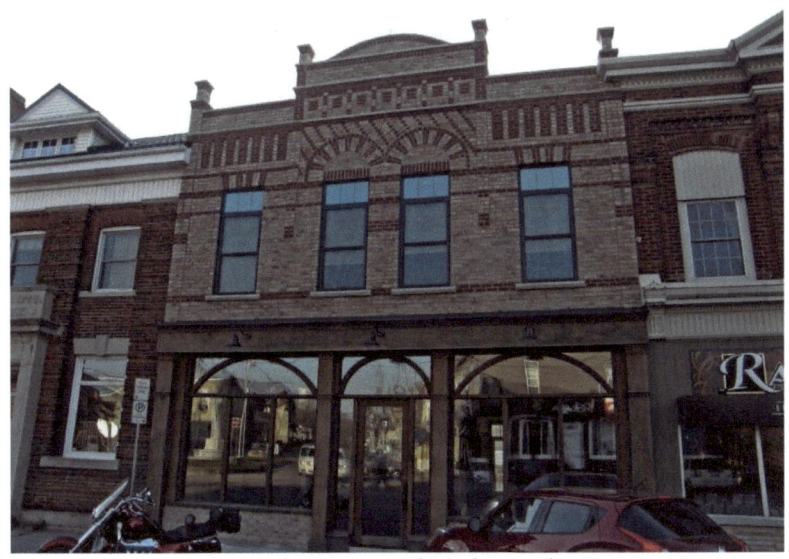

Dichromatic brickwork

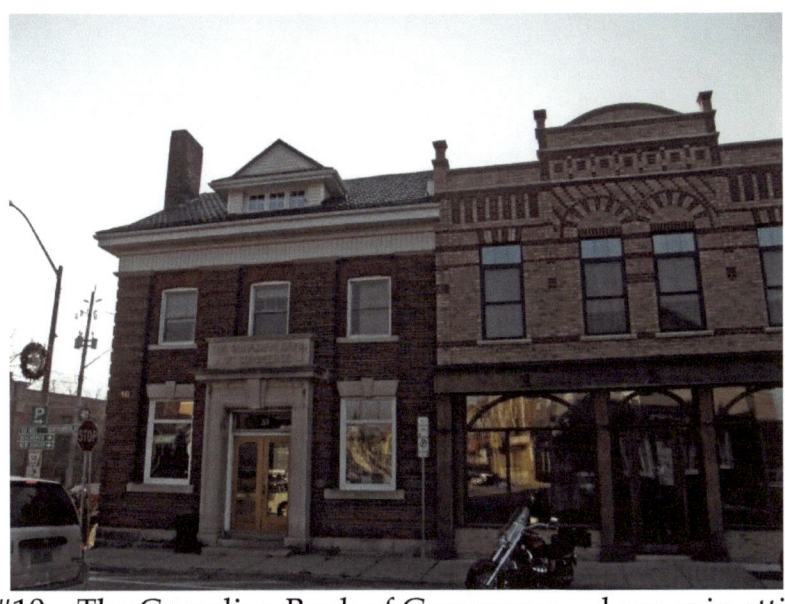

#10 – The Canadian Bank of Commerce – dormer in attic

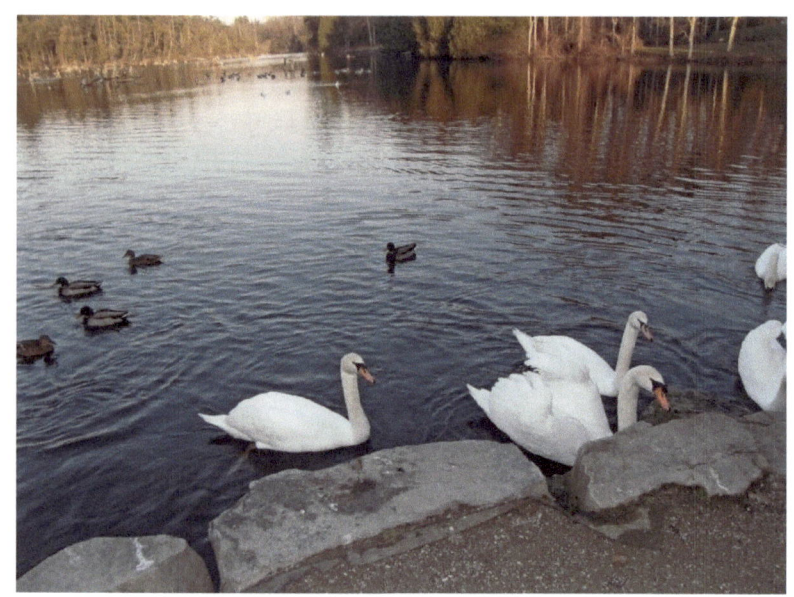

Swans and ducks at Jedburgh Dam

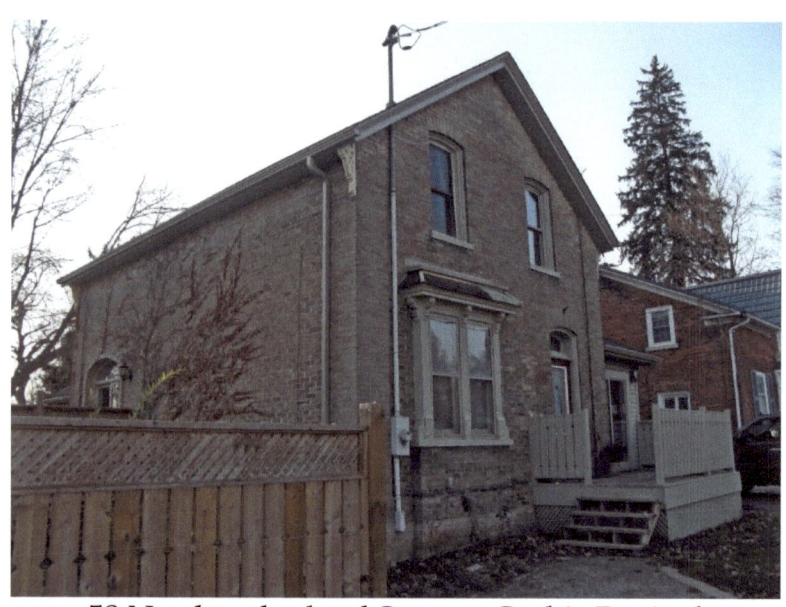

58 Northumberland Street – Gothic Revival

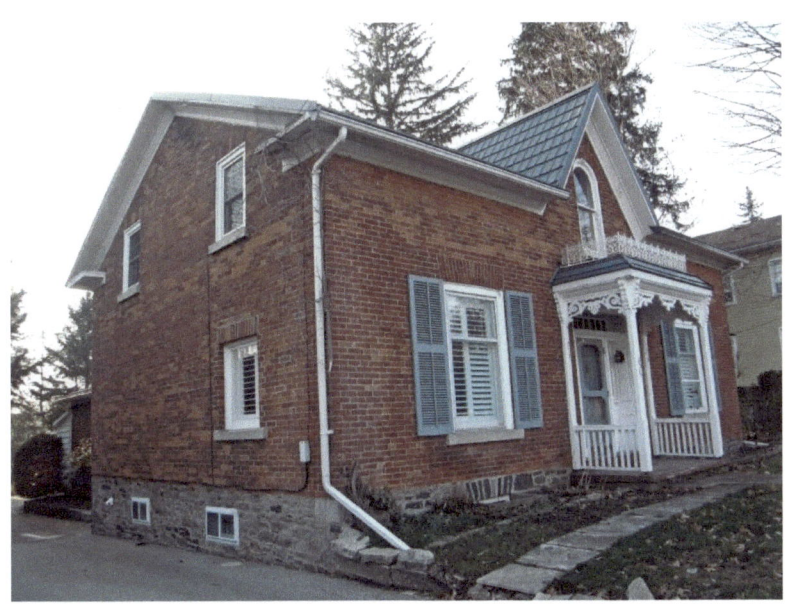

60 Northumberland Street – Gothic Revival,
Iron cresting above the entranceway

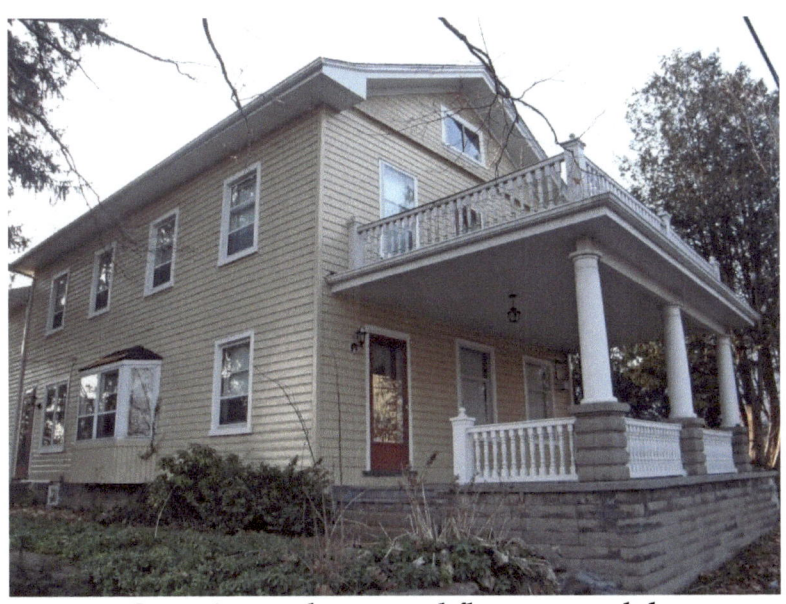

Georgian style, second floor verandah

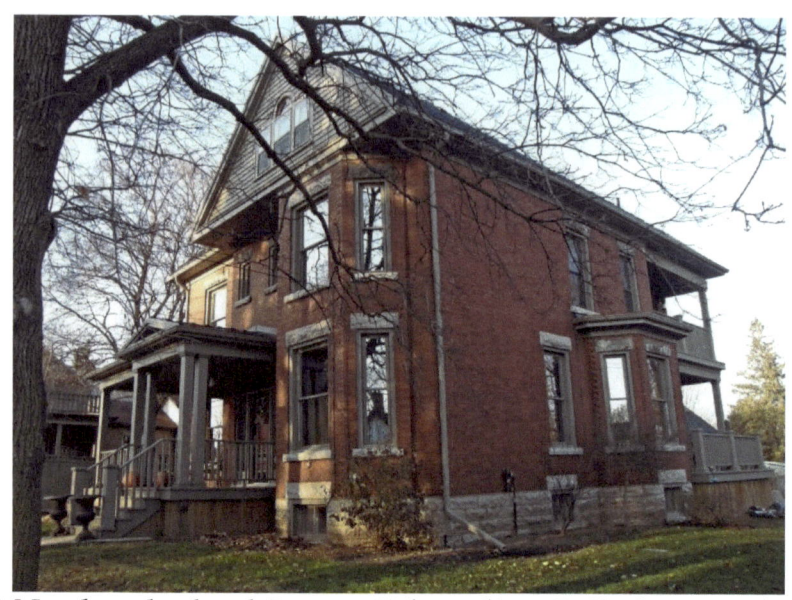

81 Northumberland Street – Edwardian, Palladian window, red brick, Two-storey bay window on front, pediment above porch, bay window on side

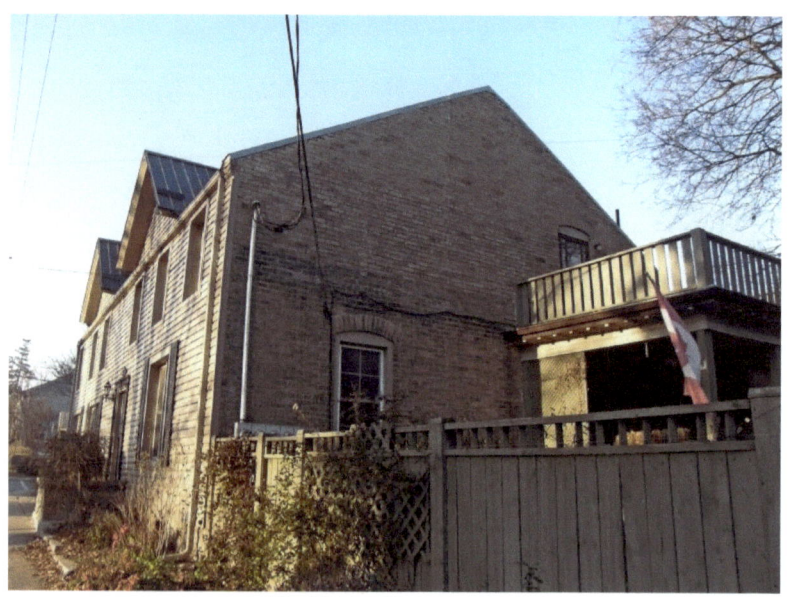

Gothic - limestone

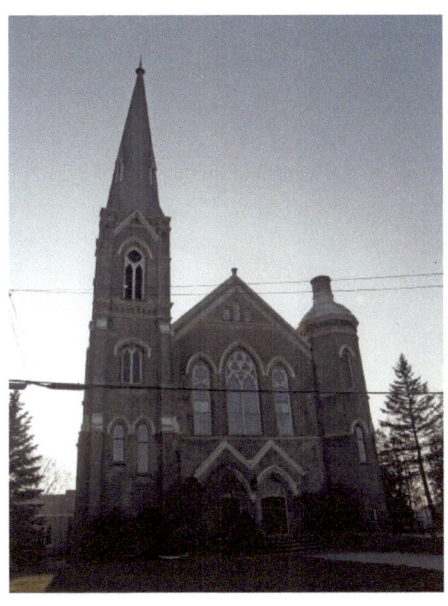

Knox United Church
92 Northumberland Street

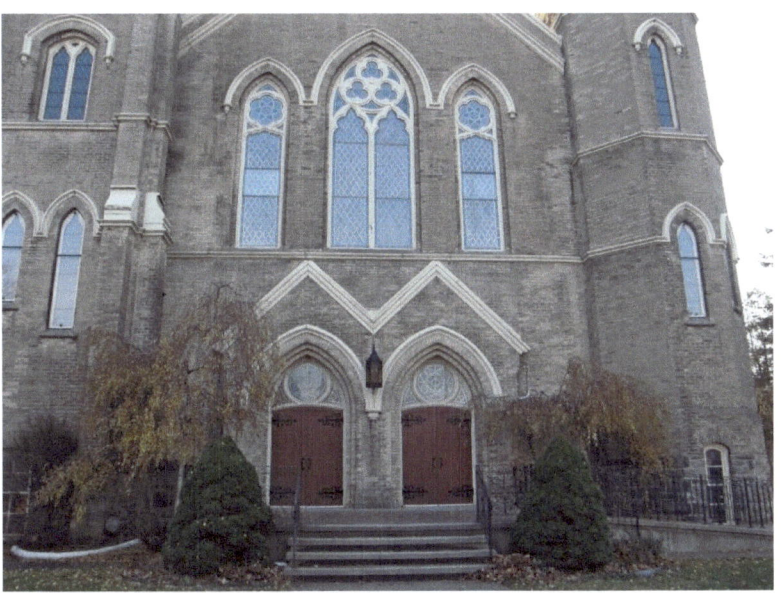

Lancet windows on tower

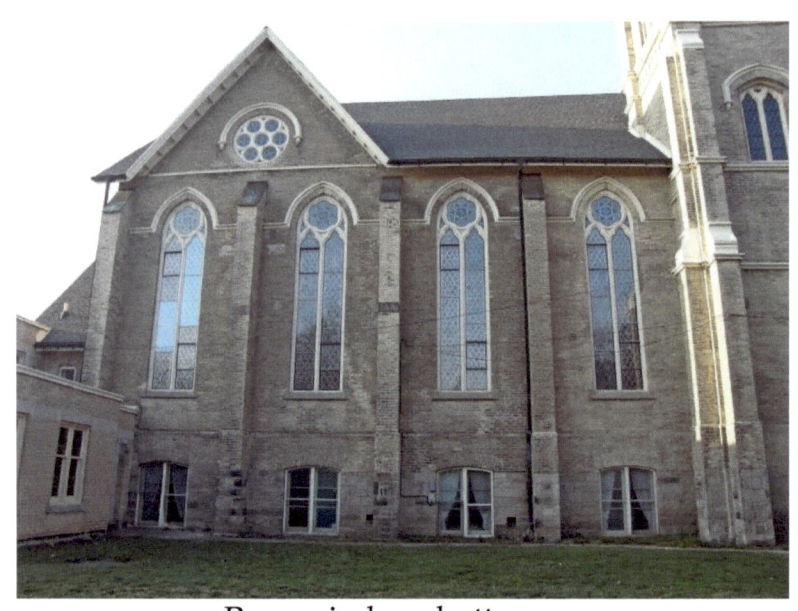

Rose window, buttresses

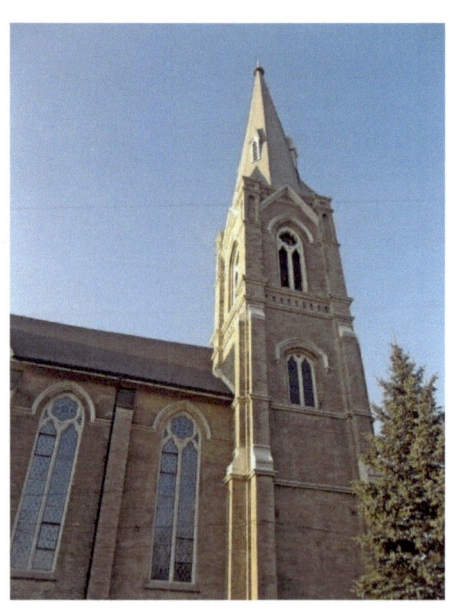

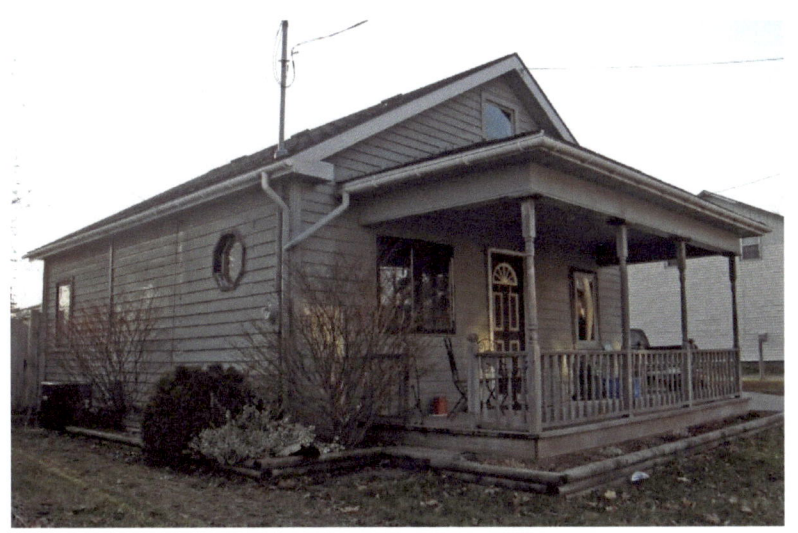

100 Northumberland Street

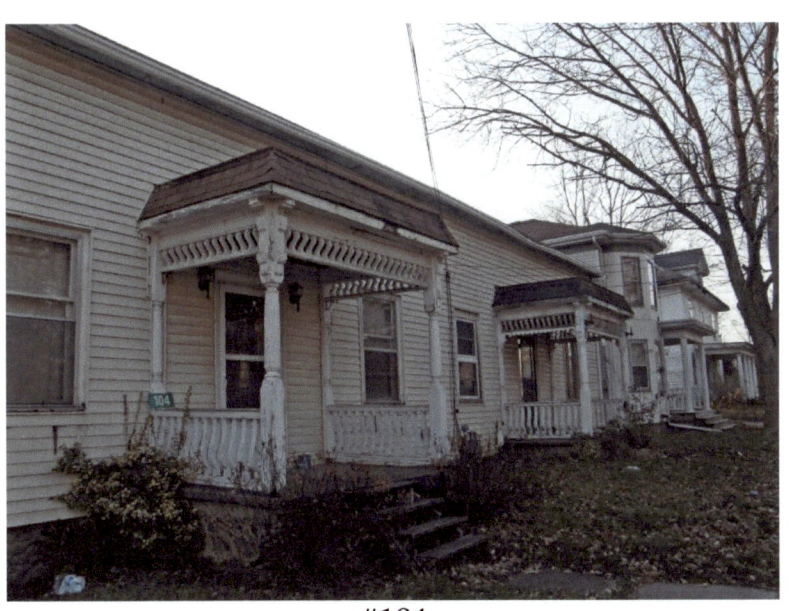

#104

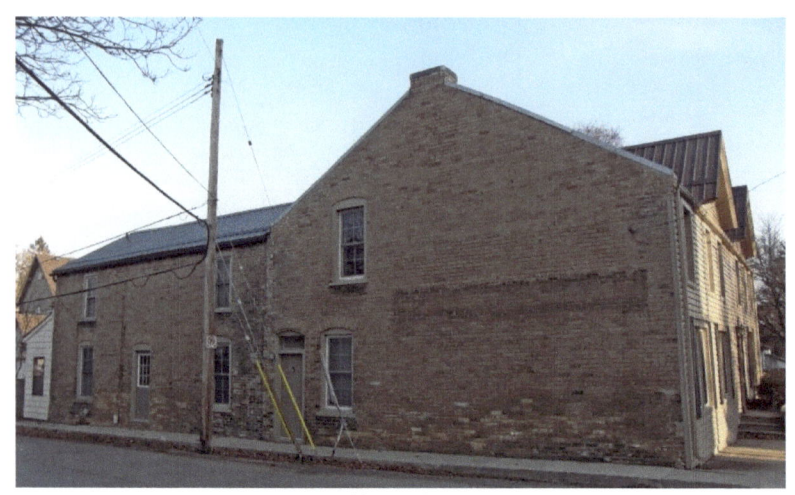

Yellow brick

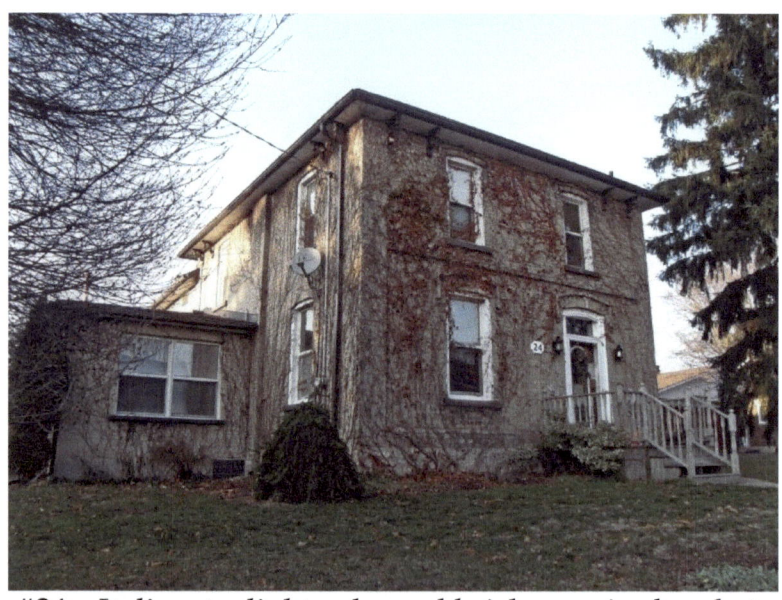

#24 – Italianate, light coloured brick, cornice brackets

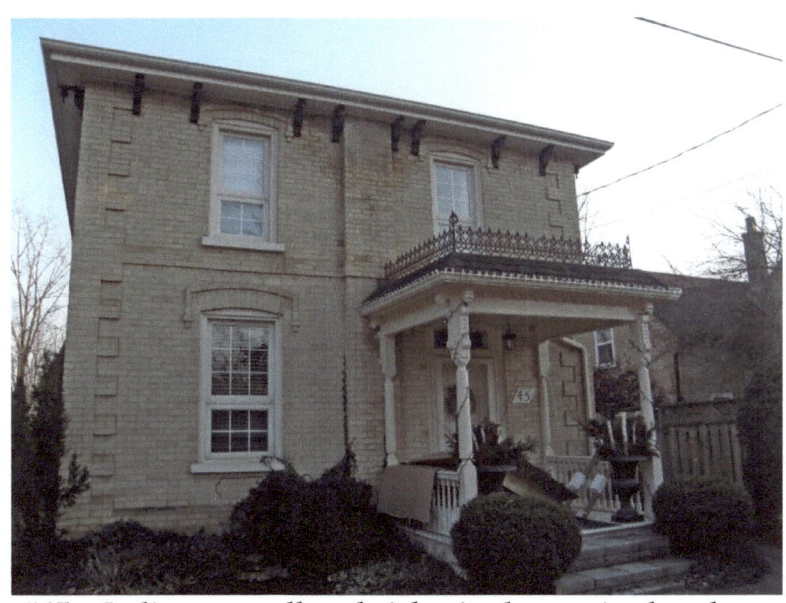

#45 – Italianate, yellow brick, single cornice brackets, iron cresting above entranceway, corner quoins

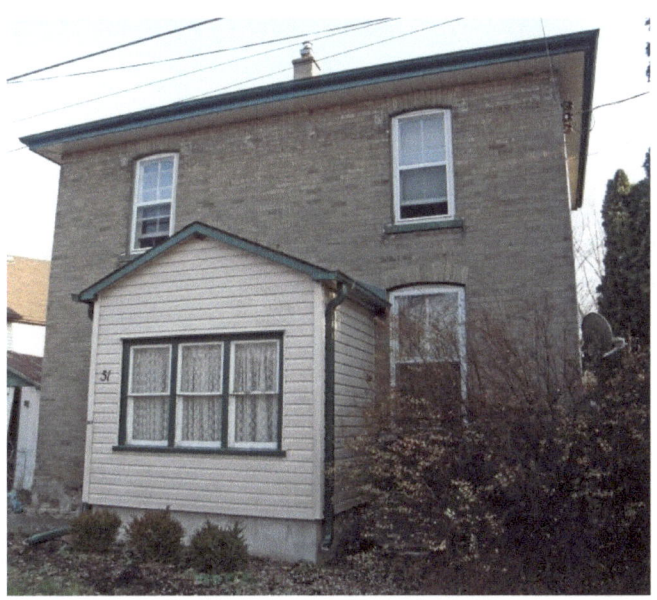

Italianate, yellow brick

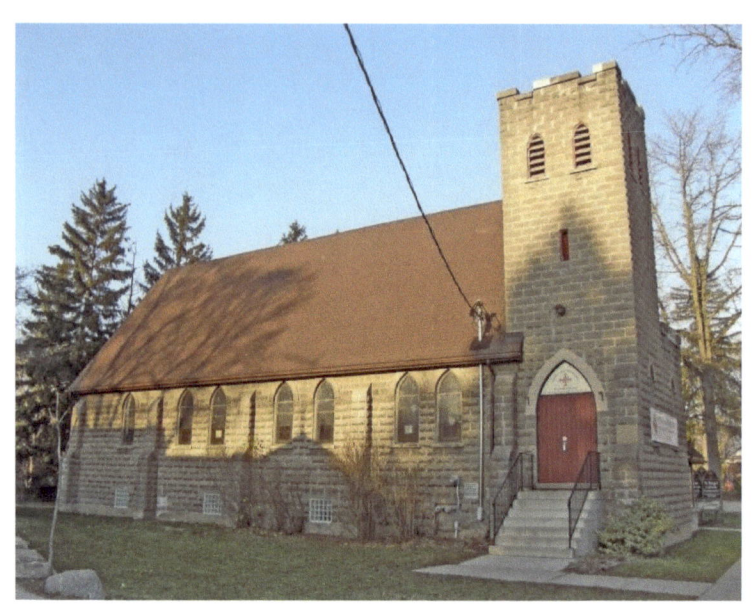

50 Manley Street - Christ Anglican Church
Celebrating 100 years – 1912-2012

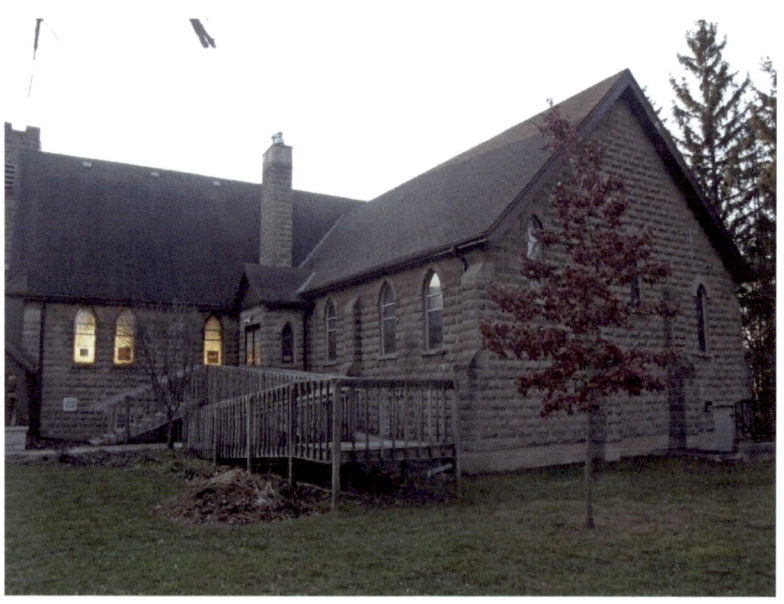

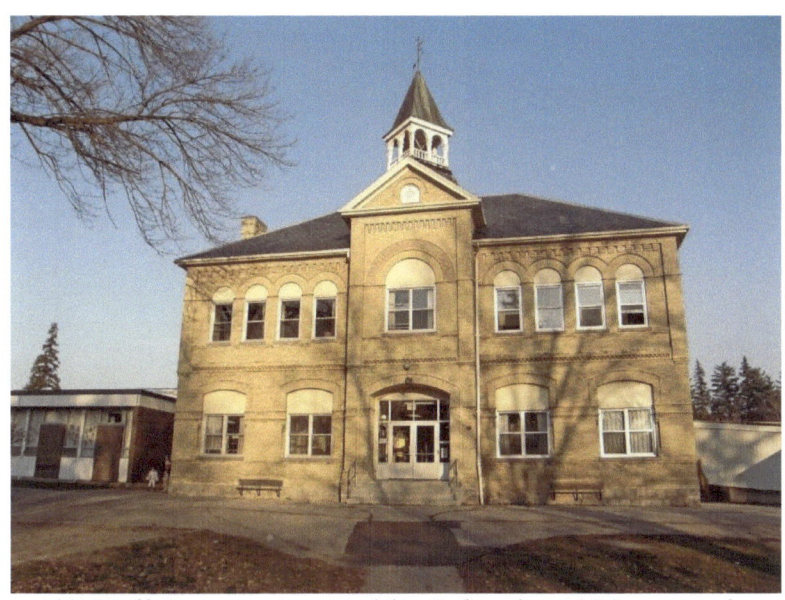

105 Hall Street - Ayr Public School – 1890 – cupola,
Romanesque style window arches, dentil moulding

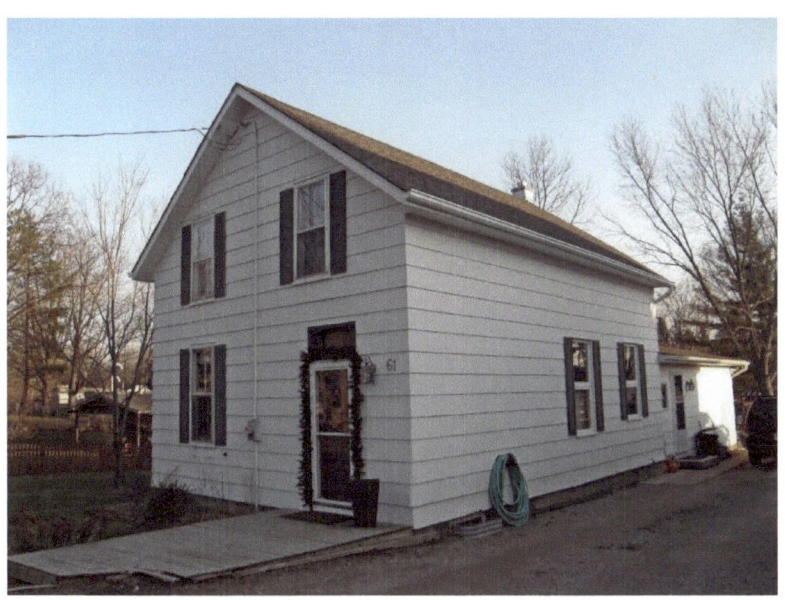

#61 McDonald Street - Gothic

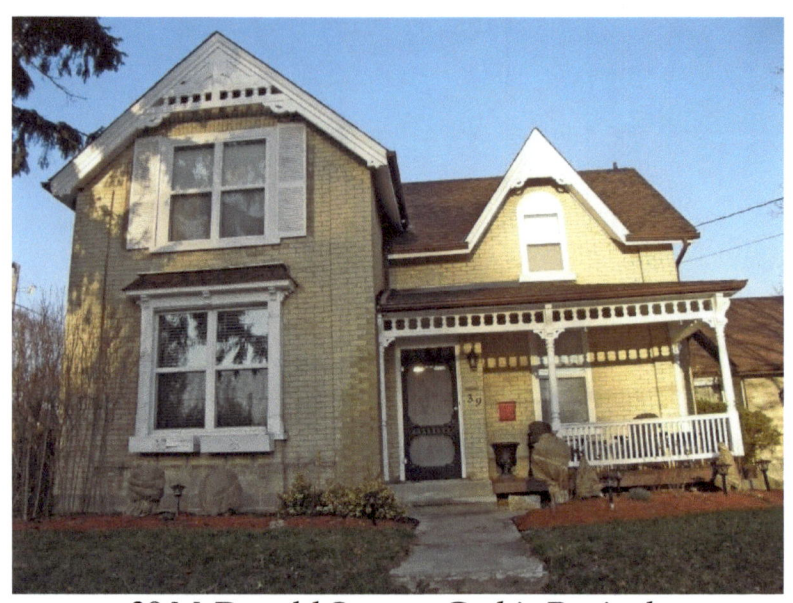

39 McDonald Street – Gothic Revival,
verge board trim on gables

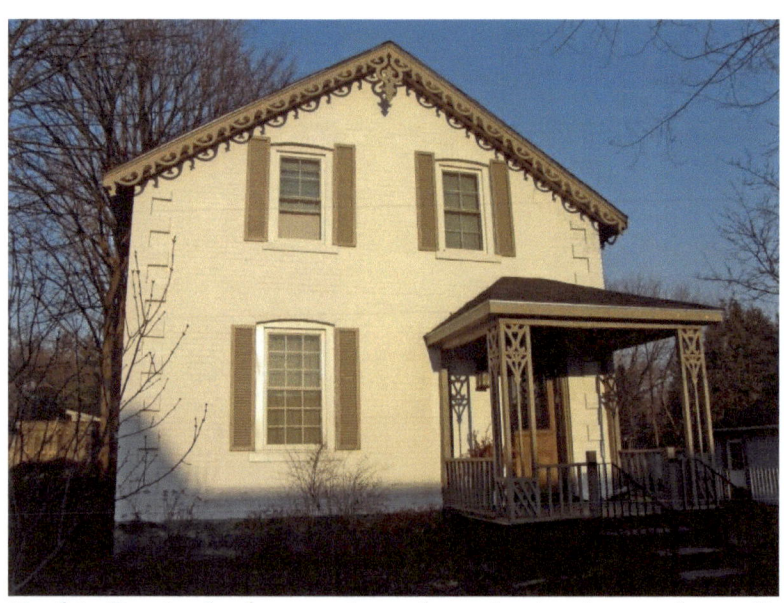

Gothic Revival - fancy gingerbread trim (verge board),
corner quoins

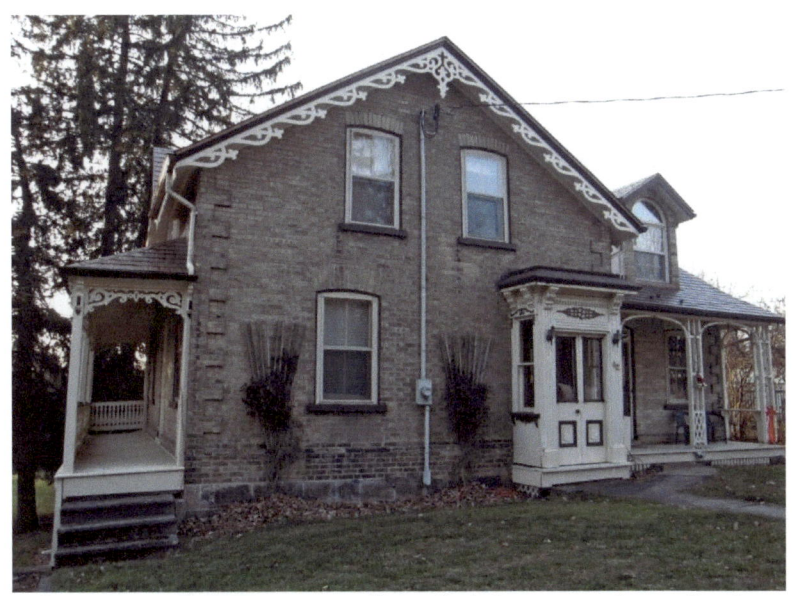

42 McDonald Street – yellow brick, verge board trim, corner quoins

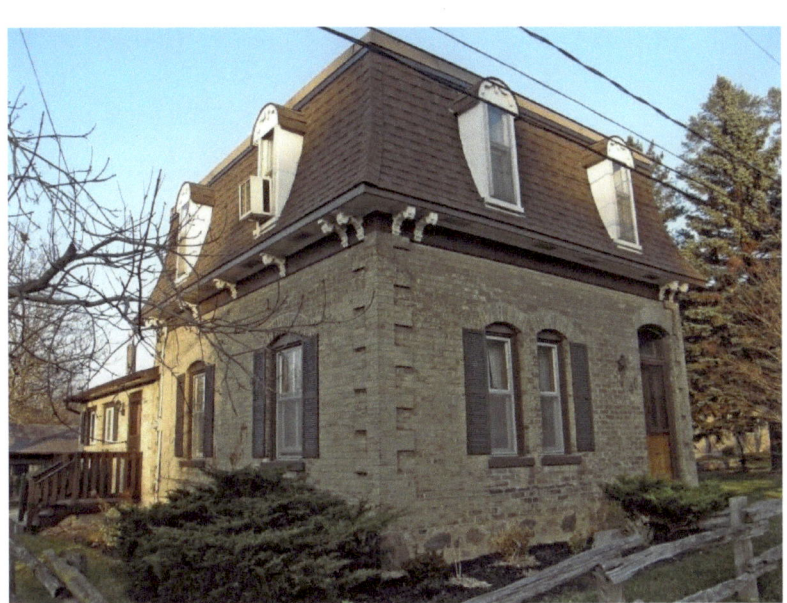

40 McDonald Street – Second Empire style, mansard roof with dormers, yellow brick, cornice brackets, corner quoins

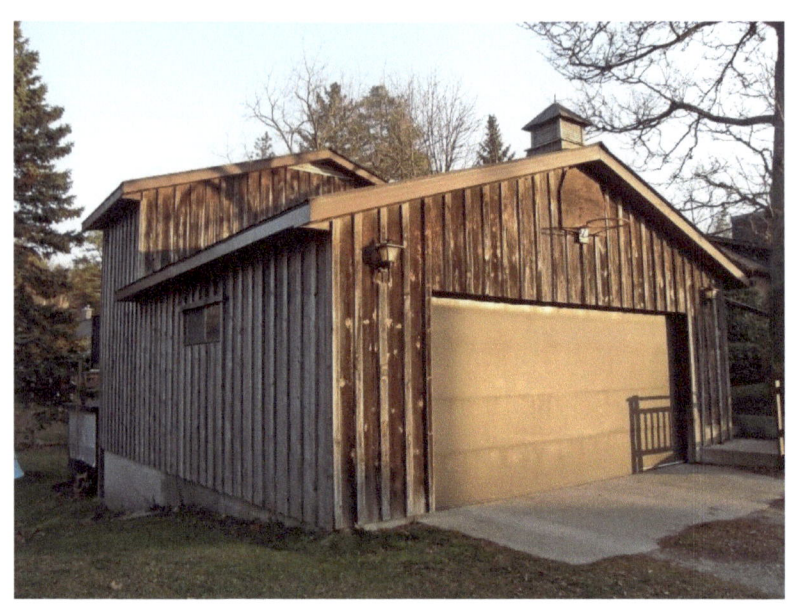

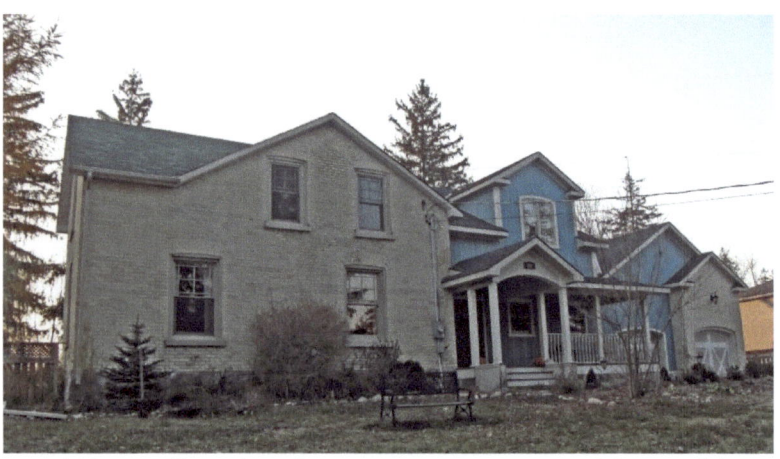

#142 – yellow brick – cornice return on blue gable

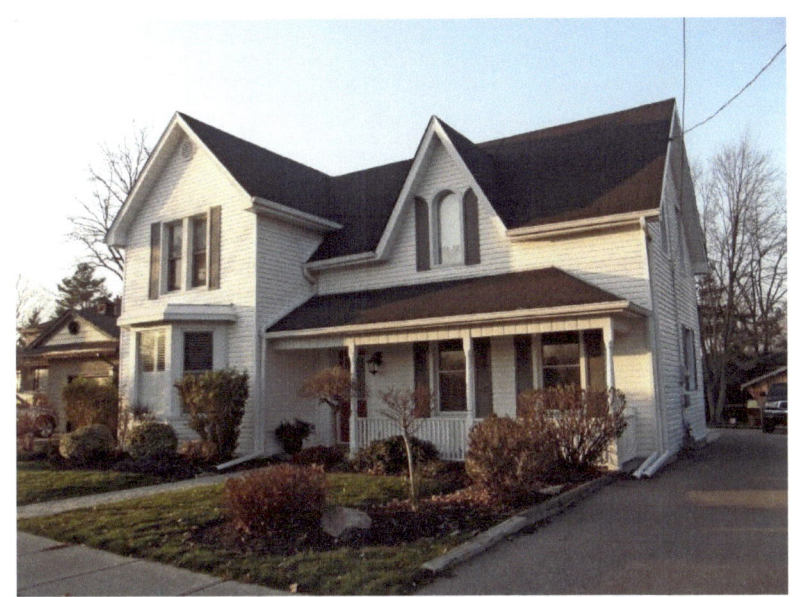

158 Main Street – Gothic Revival

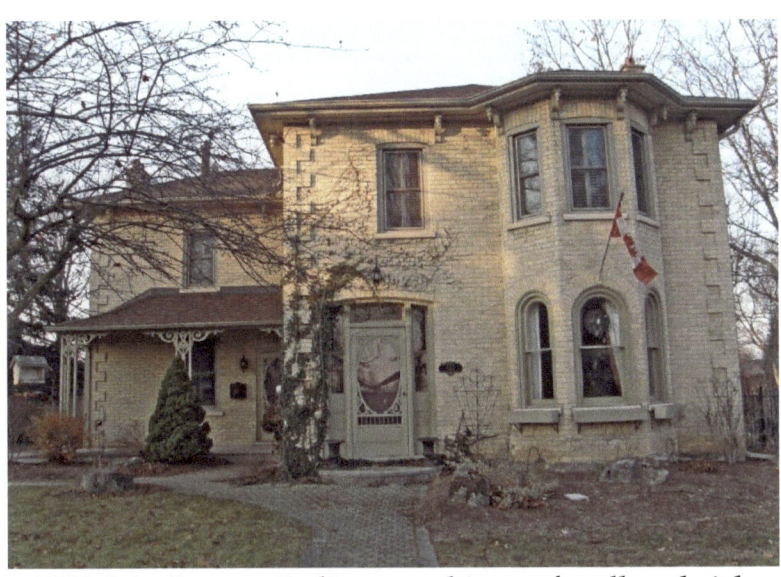

102 Main Street – Italianate – hip roof, yellow brick, two-storey bay window, corner quoins, cornice brackets

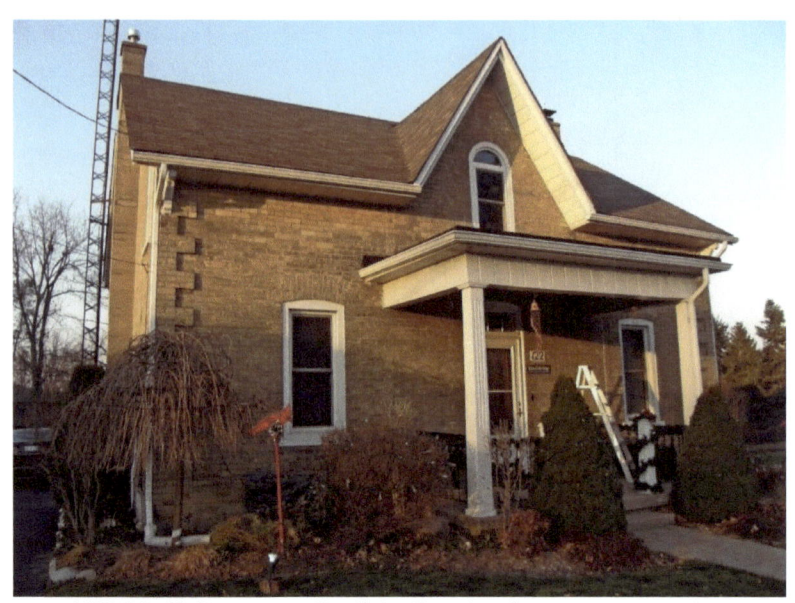

122 Hall Street – Gothic Revival, corner quoins

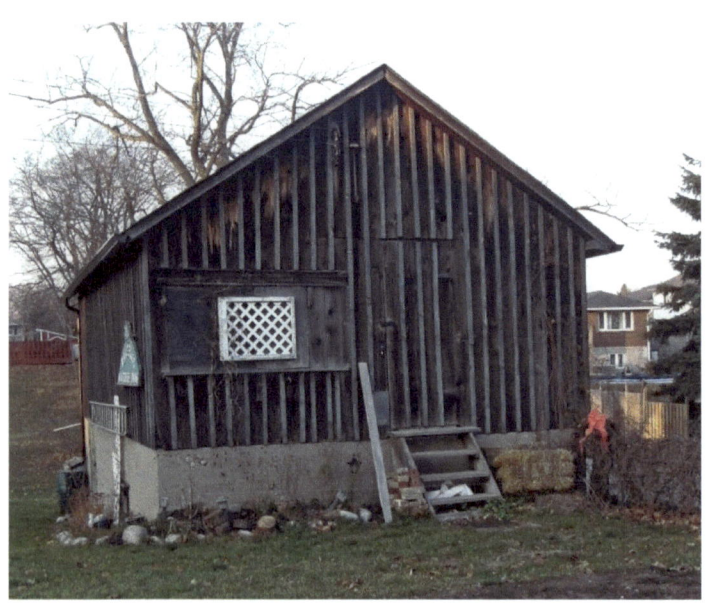

Architectural Terms

Brackets: a decorative or weight-bearing structural element which forms a right angle with one side against a wall and the other under a projecting surface such as an eave or roof. Example: see Page 27	
Buttress: a masonry structure built against or projecting from a wall which serves to support or reinforce the wall. In Canadian architecture, they are sometimes used for decoration. Example: Knox United Church	
Cobblestone architecture: Refers to the use of cobblestones embedded in mortar as a method for erecting walls on houses and commercial buildings. Example: see Page 15	
Cornice: originally the wooden overhang of the roof. With the use of stone, brick, iron and steel, the cornice is any projecting shelf at the top of a ceiling or roof. They can be very decorative. Example: see Page 34	
Cornice Return: decorative element on the end of a gable. Example: see Page 18	
Cupola: A domed or curved roof rising from a building as a decorative element. Example: Ayr Public School	
Dentil Moulding: an even series of rectangles used as ornamental decoration in cornices. Example: Stanley Street, see Page 11	

Dichromatic brickwork: the use of two colours of brick, tile or slate to decorate a façade. Example: see Page 15	
Dormer: (French for "sleep") a gable end window that pierces through the plane of a sloping roof surface to create usable space in the top floor or attic of a building by adding headroom. Example: see Page 19	
Gable: the triangular portion of a wall between the edges of a sloping roof. Example: see Page 8	
Iron Cresting: A decorative ornament along the top of a roof. Iron cresting was popular in the Baroque era and also in Italianate, Victorian, Second Empire and Queen Anne styles of architecture. Example: see Page 8	
Keystones and Voussoirs: a voussoir is a wedge-shaped element used in building an arch. A keystone is the central stone that locks all the stones into position, allowing the arch to bear weight. A keystone is often enlarged and embellished. Example: see Page 12	
Lancet Window: a tall, narrow window with a pointed arch at its top. Example: see Page 23	

Mansard Roof: This style was popularized by Francois Mansart (1598-1666), an accomplished architect of the French Baroque period and especially fashionable during the Second French Empire (1852-1870). This roof is almost flat on the top section, with two slopes on each of its sides with the lower slope at a steeper angle than the upper and having dormer windows. Example: 99 Stanley Street, see Page 10	
Palladian Window: a large window that is divided into three sections with the centre section larger than the two side sections and usually arched. Example: 81 Northumberland Street, Page 22	
Pediment: a triangular section above the horizontal structure (entablature), typically supported by columns. The inside of the triangle is called the tympanum. Example: see Page 22	
Pilaster: a slightly projecting column built into or applied to the face of a wall for additional structural support. Example: see Page 18	
Quoin: masonry blocks at the corner of a wall, often a decorative feature, usually larger or of a different colour than the rest of the wall. Example: see Page 27	

Rose Window: a circular window with ornamental tracery radiating from the centre. Example: see Page 24	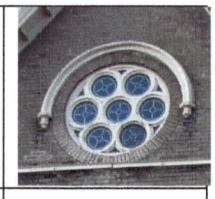
Vergeboard and Finial: also called bargeboards – hang from the projecting end of a roof and are often elaborately carved and ornamented. **Finial:** ornament added to the top of a gable, pinnacle, canopy or spire – a Gothic element. Example: see Page 30	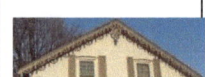

Building Styles

Edwardian, 1900-1930 – This style bridges the ornate and elaborate styles of the Victorian era and the simplified styles of the 20th century. Balanced facades, simple roof lines, dormer windows, large front porches, and smooth brick surfaces are its characteristics. Example: 81 Northumberland Street, Page 22	
Georgian, before 1860 – This style began with the British King Georges in the 18th century. These buildings have balanced facades around a central door, medium-pitched gable roofs, and small paned windows. Example: see Page 21	
Gothic Revival, 1830-1890 – These decorative buildings have sharply-pitched gables with highly detailed vergeboards, pointed-arch window openings, and dichromatic brickwork. It is a common style in Ontario. Example: see Page 30	
Italianate, 1850-1900 – It has wide-bracketed eaves, belvederes, wrap-around verandahs. Example: see Page 7	

Neo-Classical (1810 - 1850) – This style was a direct result of the War of 1812. Many Upper Canadians returning from the war with the United States were second or third generation Loyalists who had inherited land and means from their forefathers. Once the conflict had passed, they had the money and the time to expand their holdings and indulge their architectural whims. Both residential and commercial buildings were constructed on the traditional Georgian plan, but they had a new gaiety and light-heartedness. Detailing became more refined, delicate, and elegant. Example: Library – see Page 6	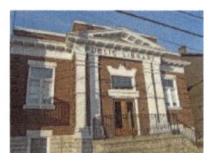
Romanesque Revival, 1880-1910 – This style hearkens back to medieval architecture of the 11th and 12th centuries with a heavy appearance, blocky towers and rounded arches. Example: Ayr Public School, Page 29	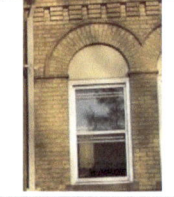
Second Empire, 1860-1880 – The mansard roof is the most noteworthy feature of this style and is evidence of the French origins. Projecting central towers and one or two-storey bays can also be present. Example: see Page 10	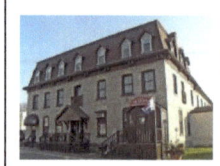